THE PERSONAL FINANCE APPLICATION

HOW TO SAVE MONEY

EMILIO ALEU

AuthorHouse™
1663 Liberty Drive
Bloomington, IN 47403
www.authorhouse.com
Phone: 833-262-8899

Published by AuthorHouse 02/17/2023

ISBN: 978-1-5246-5802-1 (sc)
ISBN: 978-1-5246-5801-4 (e)

Overview: Example of Some Screens

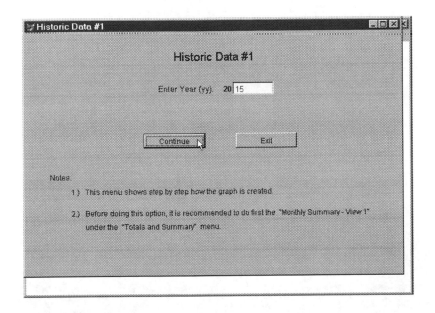

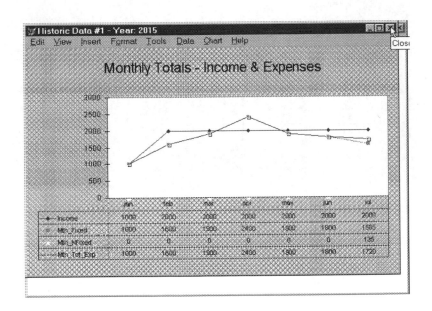

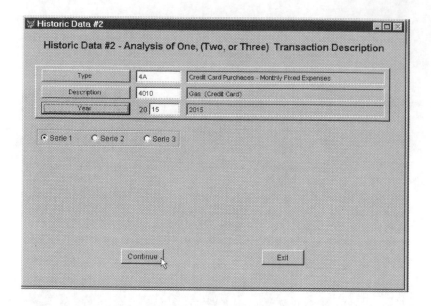

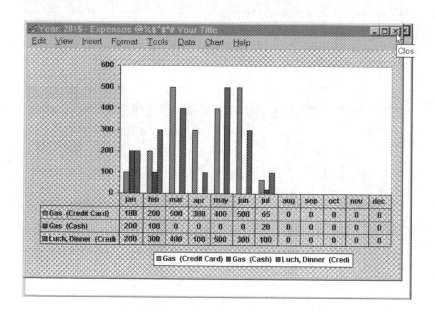

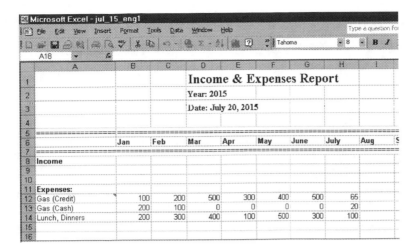

Note: The screen above illustrates an example of a report. It is an old version of Excel.

	A	B	C	D	E	F	G	H
1		Jan	Feb	Mar	Apr	May	Jun	Jul
2	Gas	10	20	30	40	50	60	70
3	Series 2	100	300	200	600	400		
4	Series 3	1000	2000	3000	4000	5000		
5	Series 4	50	800	200	500	800		
6	Series 5	400	300	200	100	300		
7	Series 6	1000	2000	4000	3000	1000		
8								
9								
10								

Example of a data to create a graph of six series.

1.) Option of creating Excel files in the screens of the Inquiry Menu. (See pages: viii, ix, xi.)
2.) Option of creating Excel files after "File/Exit" is selected. (See page viii.)
3.) Option of copying the Excel files to the USB drive after "File/Exit" is selected. (See page viii.)

Note: After the Excel files were copied to the USB, they can be used in another computer with printer to print the reports, also the Excel files can be copied to the "Drive One", ("Cloud"), using the "Drive One" Upload command, (Windows 10), then use Excel Online, (Office 365), to create and modify the reports.

Microsoft, Windows, Excel, Office 365 are either registered trademarks or trademarks of Microsoft Corporation.

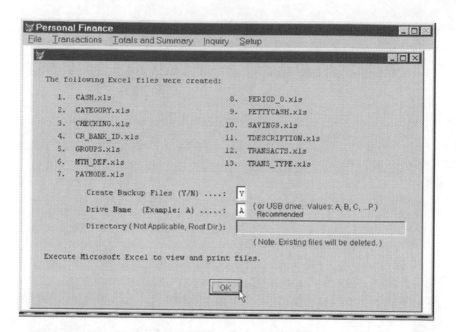

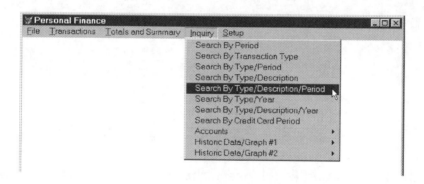

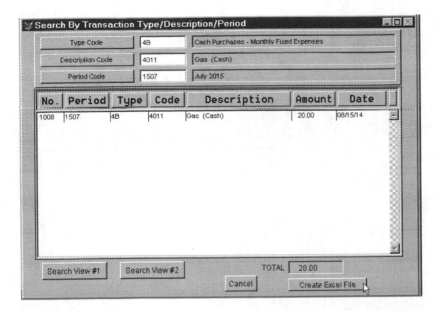

Note: The created Excel files contain all the fields of the original file. It may be necessary to delete the fields that are not required, adjust the fields column width, format fonts, add headings, etc.

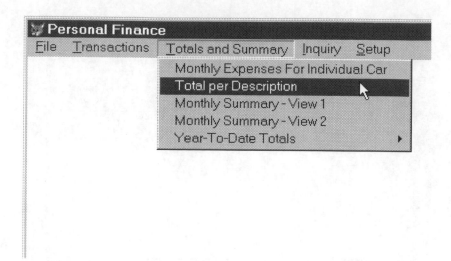

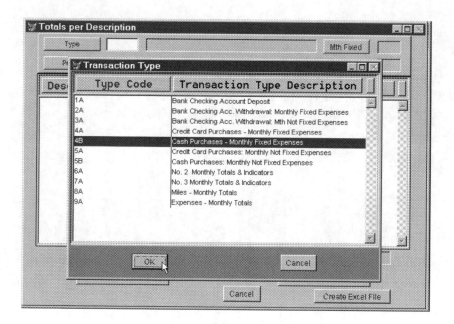

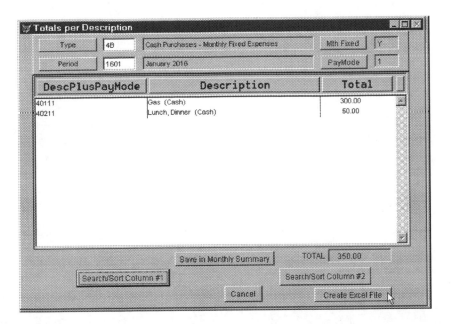

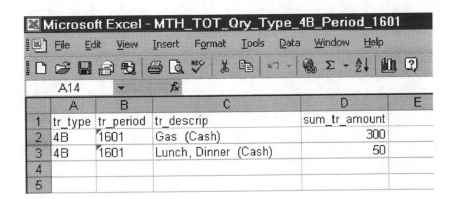

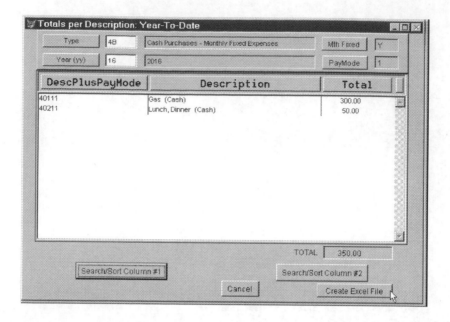

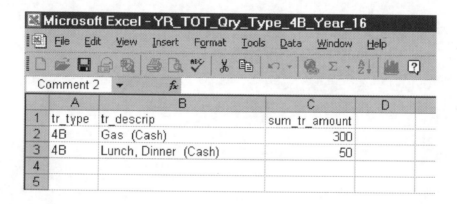

Contents

1 - Installation (English Version)

Note: The installation is not available for this version of the book. The installation is included in the version of the book THE PERSONAL FINANCE APPLICATION published on 09/25/2019. Also, Search in Google: http://www.jtmp2000.com

2 - Starting the Application

Open the C:\PFINANCE folder and select the **pfinance.exe** application.
Then do a double click with the mouse.

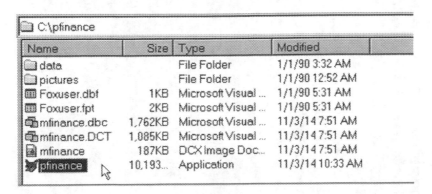

Do a click on the Command Button with the picture as shown below.

Do a click on the Command Button with the picture as shown below.

3 - The Setup Menu

Menu – Month Definition

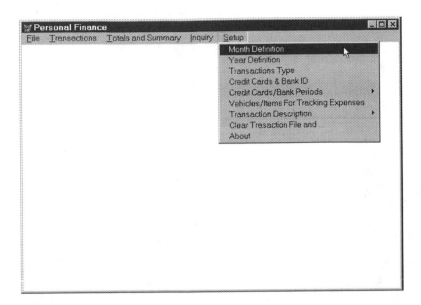

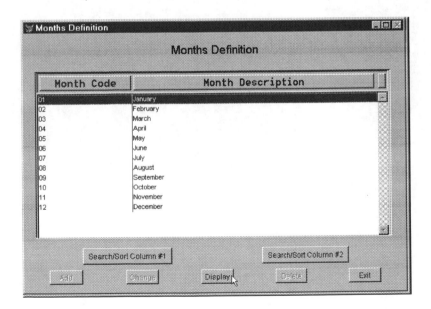

Note: This chapter is on Internet.

4 - The Transaction Menu

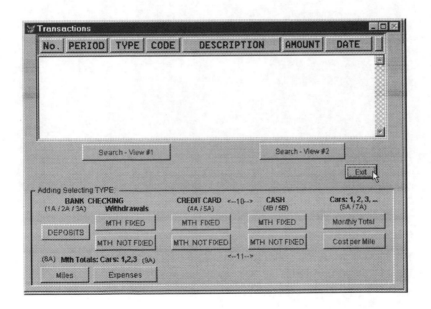

Note: This chapter is on Internet.

5 - The Checking Account and Cash Menu

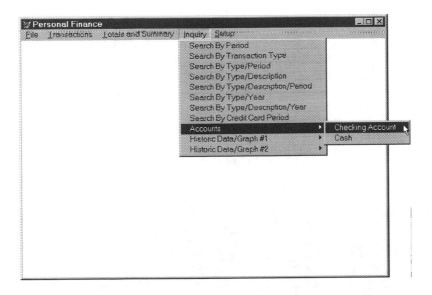

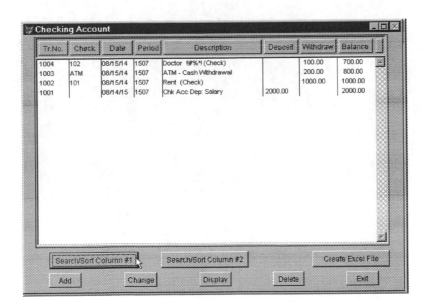

Note: This chapter is on Internet.

6 - Monthly and Year-To-Date Totals, Summary Report

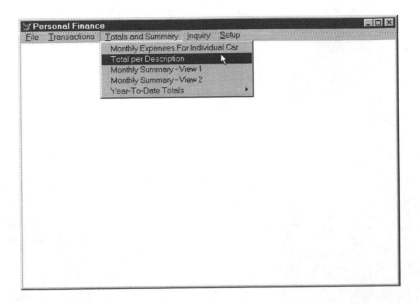

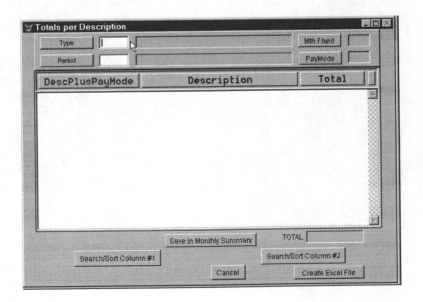

Note: This chapter is on Internet.

7 - The Inquiry Menu

Menu – Search by Period

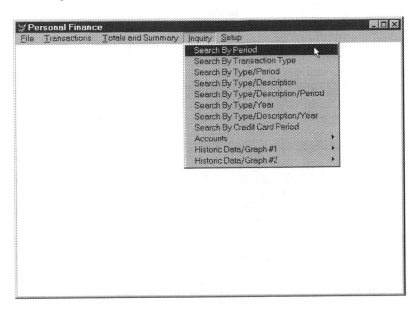

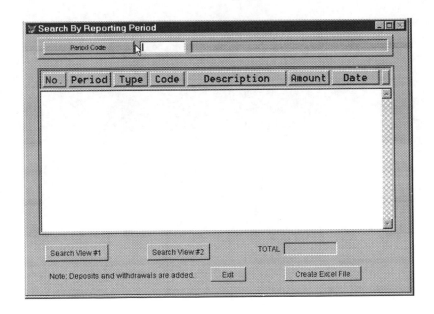

Note: This chapter is on Internet.

8 - Historic Data and Graphs

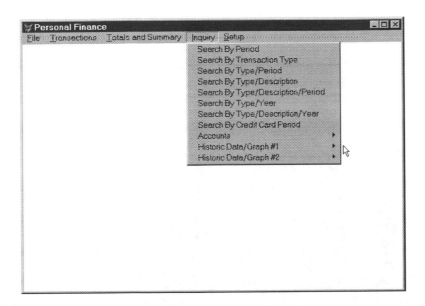

Menu-Historic Data and Graph #1-View #1

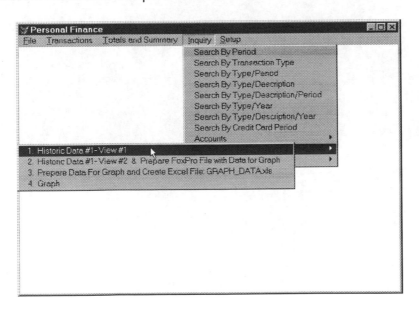

Note: This chapter is on Internet.

9 – Creating Graphs For: Monthly Car Mileage, Car Expenses and Total Cost per Mile

(Version 5.0)

I – Procedure for Creating Graphs For Monthly Car Miles

1 - The following Transaction Descriptions are already created:

8010	Car 01: Odometer Miles
8020	Car 02: Odometer Miles
8030	Car 03: Odometer Miles
8110	Car 01: Miles – Monthly Total
8120	Car 02: Miles – Monthly Total
8130	Car 03: Miles – Monthly Total

2 - The monthly car miles are obtained by subtracting the car mileage obtained at the end of the last day of the month, from the car mileage obtained at the end of the last day of the previous month.

3 - The procedure to create the graph is similar to the procedure Car 01: Odometer - Miles. See Section III.

II – Procedure for Creating Graphs For Monthly Total Car Expenses

1 - The following Transaction Descriptions are already created:

9010	Car 01: Expenses Monthly Total
9020	Car 02: Expenses Monthly Total
9030	Car 03: Expenses Monthly Total

2 - See Chapter 10 for an example of how to obtain the monthly total car expenses and how to enter a transaction.

3 - The procedure to create the graph is similar to the procedure for Monthly Car Mileage. See Section III.

III – Procedure for Creating Graphs For Monthly Car Mileage – Odometer

1 - The following Transaction Descriptions are already created: See the next two pictures.

8010	Car 01: Odometer Miles
8020	Car 02: Odometer Miles
8030	Car 03: Odometer Miles
8110	Car 01: Miles – Monthly Total
8120	Car 02: Miles – Monthly Total
8130	Car 03: Miles – Monthly Tota

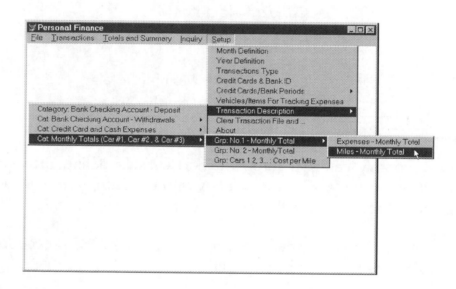

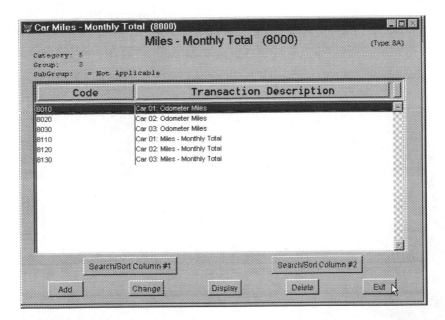

See Section 5 on page 25 for examples of Transaction Descriptions for Car Expenses and Cost per Mile.

2 - It is required to create the reporting periods before entering the transaction. See next six pictures.

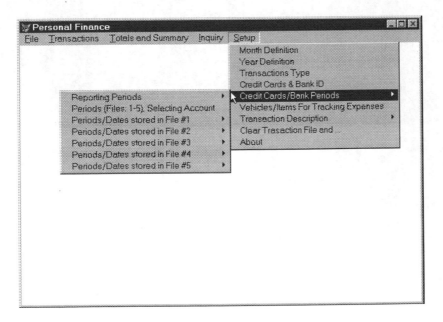

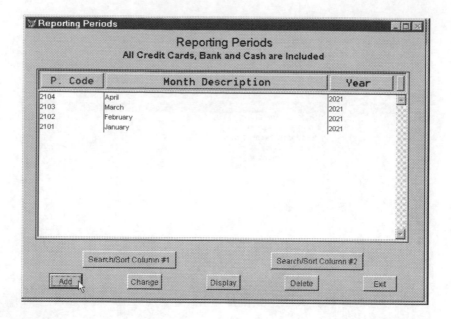

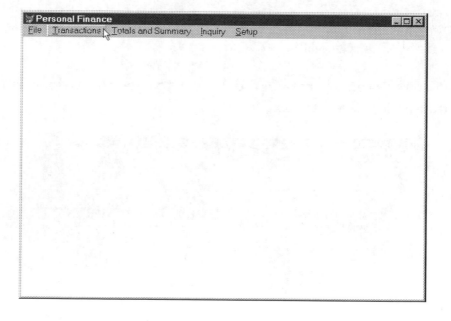

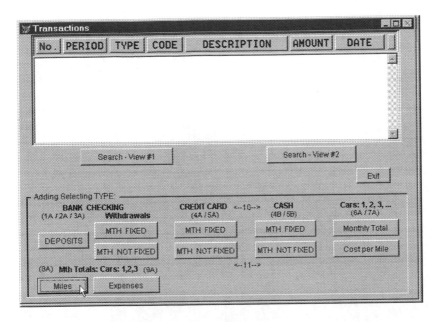

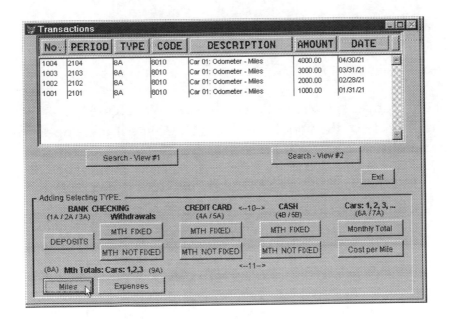

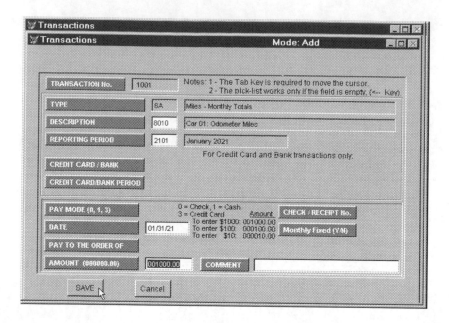

3 - Select "Historic Data/Graph #2" from the menu to create the file GRAPH_2DAT.xls, data for the graph, This is a Column Type Graph. See next four pictures.

Note: The Graph #2 is Column Type. After the file GRAPH_2DAT.xls is created, select Graph #1 from the menu, which is a Line Type, but using the file GRAPH_2DAT.xls to Import the data for the graph.

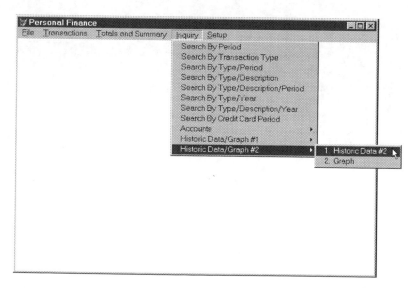

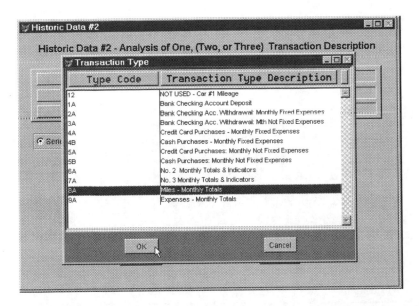

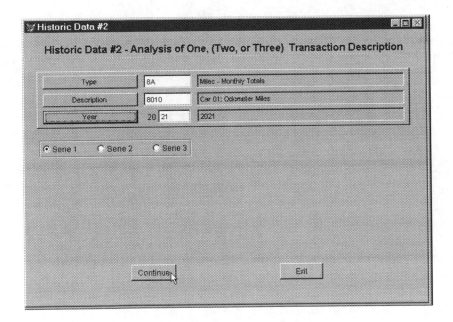

Do a click on the Continue push button to create the file GRAPH_2DAT.xls, data for the graph.

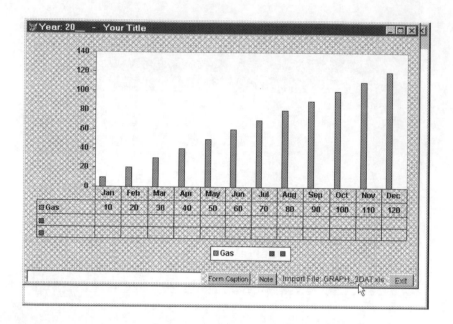

4 - Select Graph #1, (Line Type Graph), from the menu "Historic Data/Graph #1", but use GRAPH_2DAT.xls to Import File, instead of GRAPH_DAT.xls. See next seven pictures.

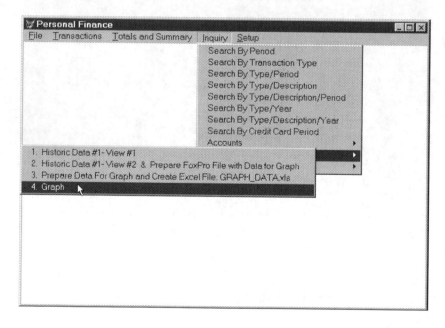

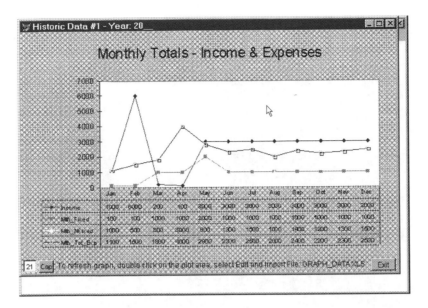

Double click on the graph plot area to edit Microsoft Graph.

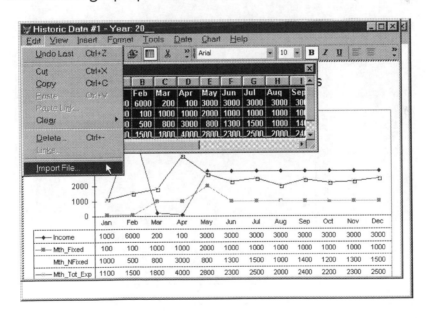

Select **Import File** from the **Edit** menu..

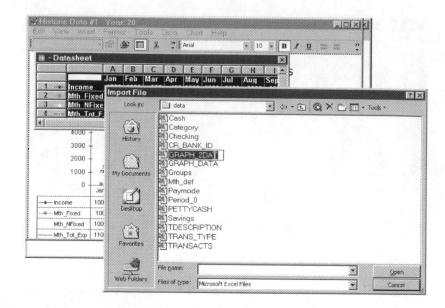

Select the GRAPH_2DAT file located in the "C:\Pfinance\data\" directory.

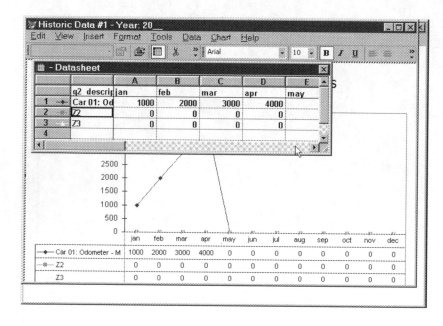

Note: This file contains the field Z2, Z3, and ceros, which can be erased with blank spaces. See the next picture.

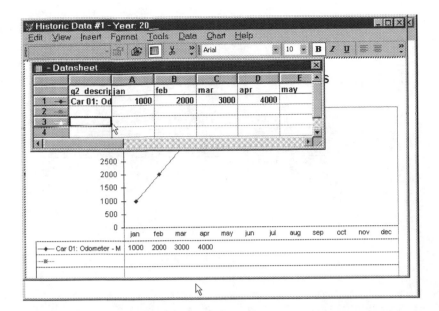

After the fields Z2, Z3, and undesired ceros are erased, do a click outside the graph to exit from the option of updating the graph.

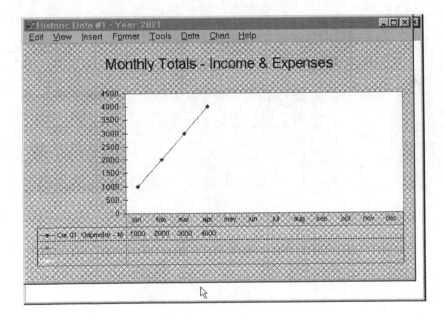

Use Microsoft Excel to copy and paste the graph.

5 - Examples of other Transaction Descriptions for Cars 1, Car 2, and Cars 3, 4, 5...

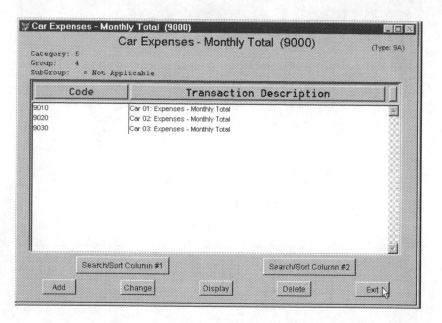

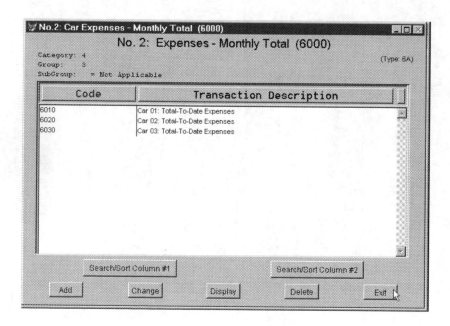

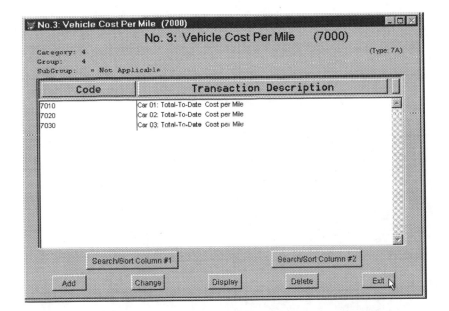

10 – Obtaining Car Expenses For Individual Car
If There Are More Than One Vehicle

(Version 5.0)

1 - Cars 1, 2, and 3 are defined in the Setup menu, under the submenu "Vehicles / Items For Tracking Expenses": See next three pictures.

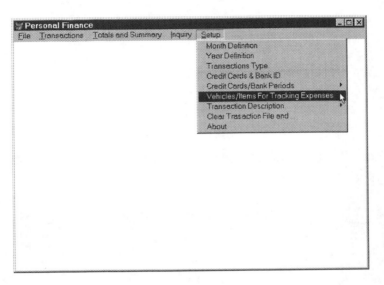

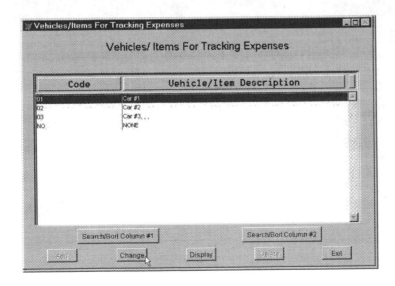

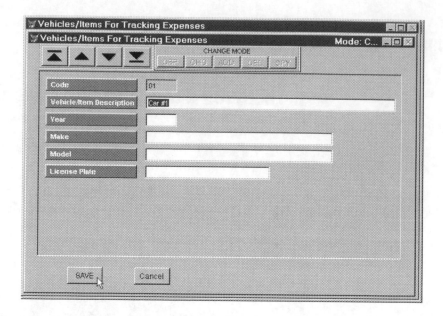

2 - The code for tracking car expenses is included in the Transaction Definition. See next four pictures.

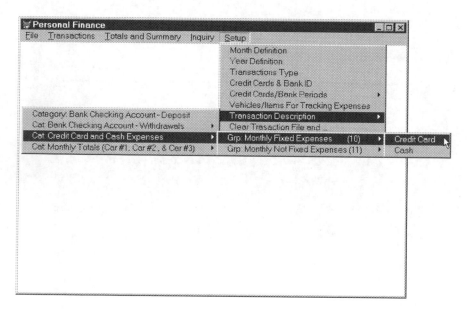

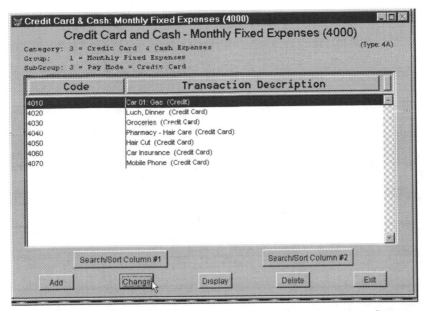

Note: Change description to: **Car 01: Gas (Credit)**

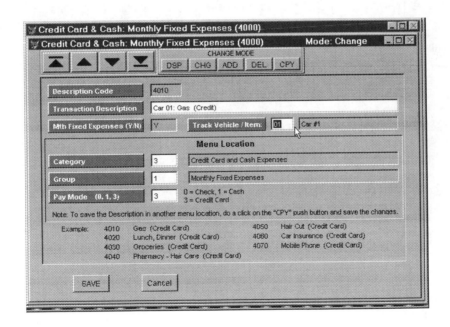

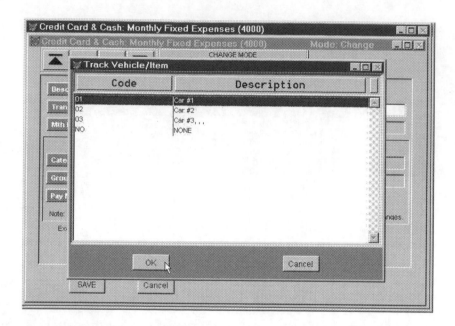

3 - If the Transaction Definition with the code for tracking expenses is included in a transaction, this will be indicated in the first line of the screen. See next five pictures.

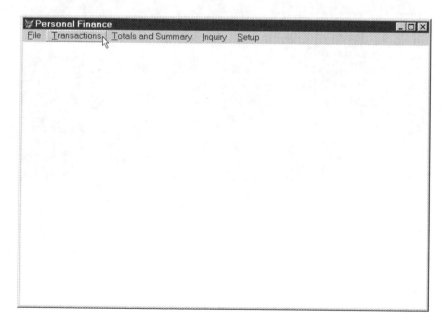

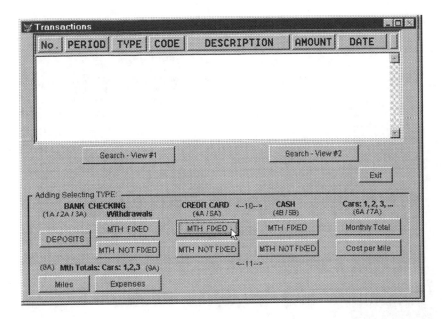

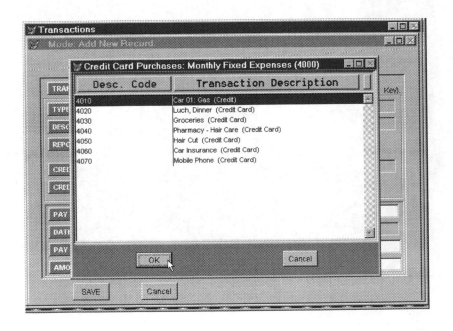

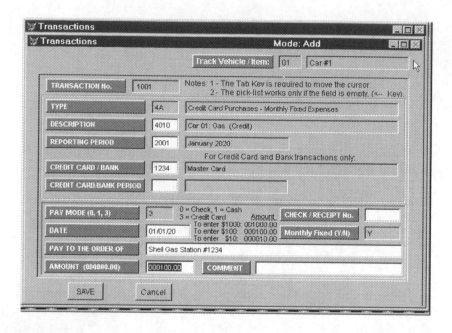

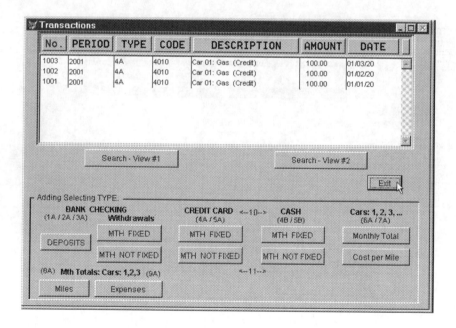

4 - To obtain the total expenses for an individual car, select the submenu "Monthly Expenses For Individual Car", under the "Totals and Summary" menu. See next three pictures.

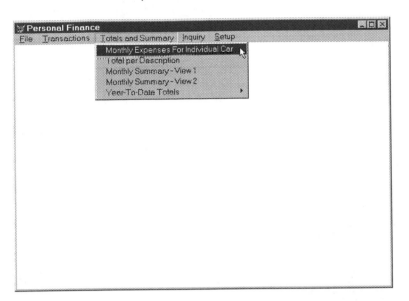

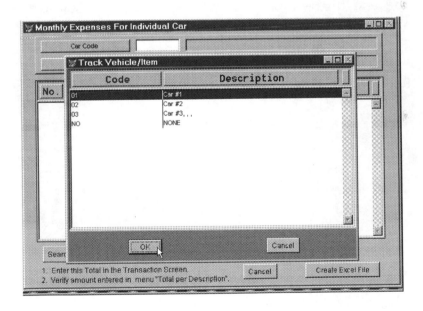

Note: If there are more than three vehicles, for example, with the following Transaction Description:

Car 03: Gas (Credit)
Car 04: Gas (Credit)
Car 05: Gas (Credit)

after creating the Excel file, (see picture below), use Microsoft Excel to sort the file and add totals.

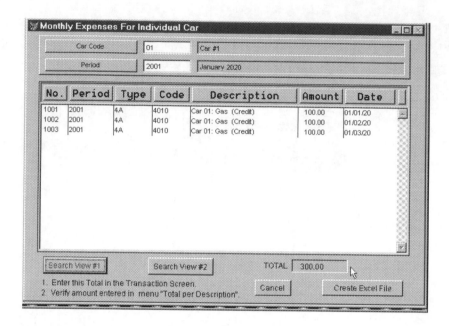

5 - At the end of the month, enter the total expenses for the car, in one transaction. See next five pictures. This is to facilitate the creation of graph, and other analysis.

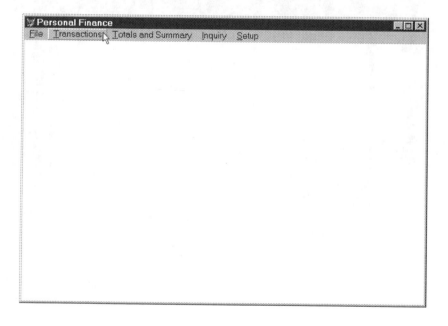

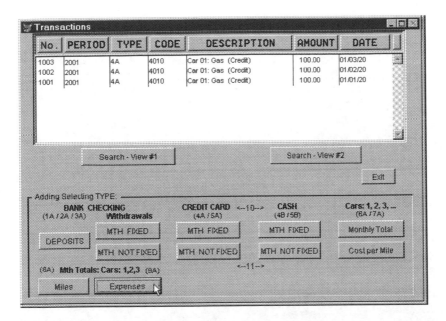

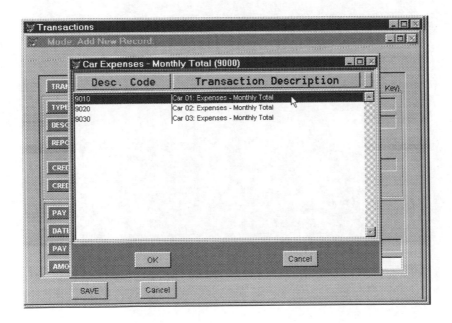

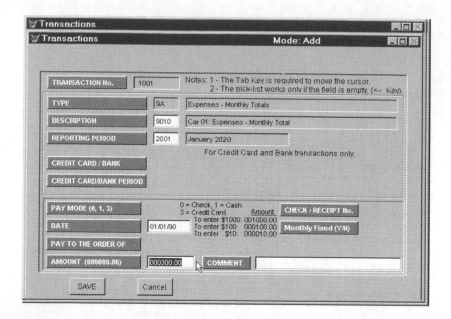

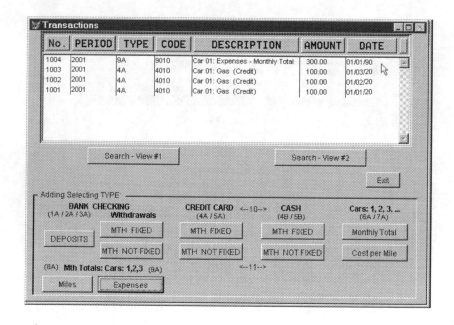

6 - To verify the transaction entered, select the "Total per Description" submenu, under the "Totals and Summary" menu. See next three pictures.

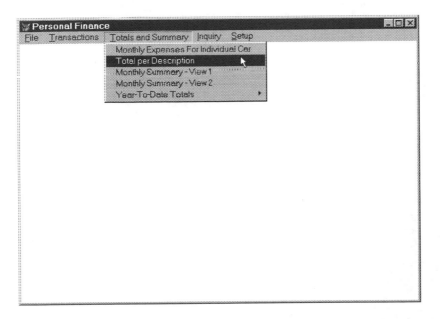

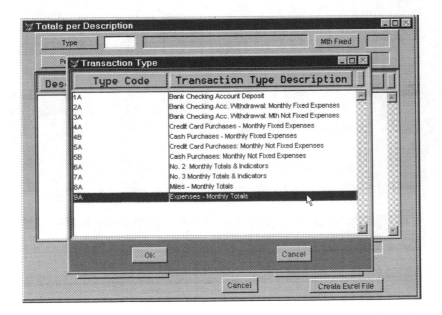

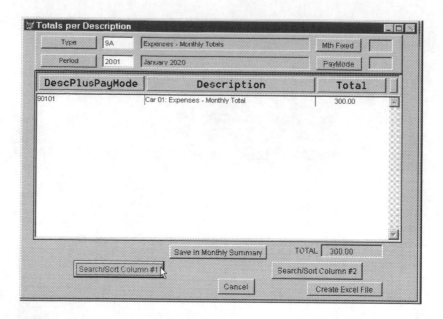

7 - Obtaining Cost per Mile and Creating Graphs

1. Use Microsoft Excel for:

   - Enter the car mileage for the month
   - Enter the car total monthly expenses
   - Calculate the total miles for the month
   - Calculate the total car expenses: Life of the car-To-Date
   - Calculate Cost per Mile

2. Enter these values in a transaction for each month using the Transaction Description already created.

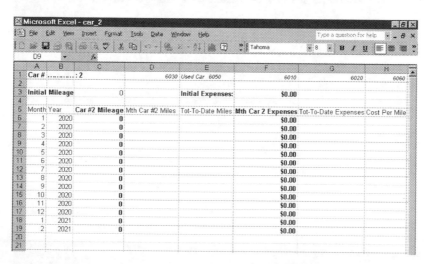

3. Creating Graphs for Cost Per Mile.

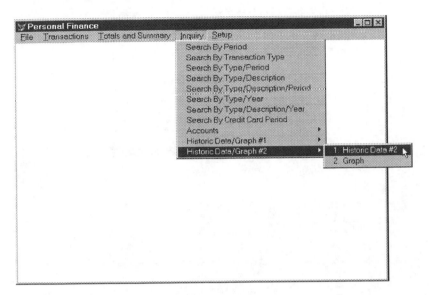

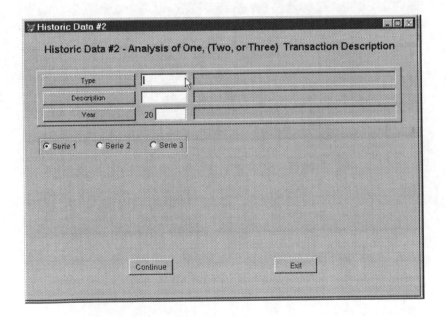

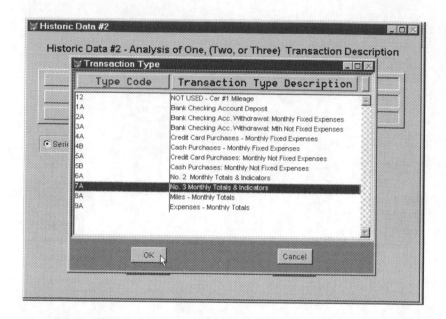

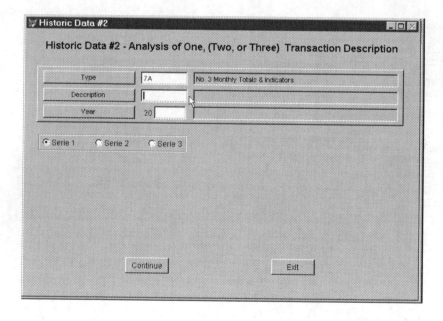

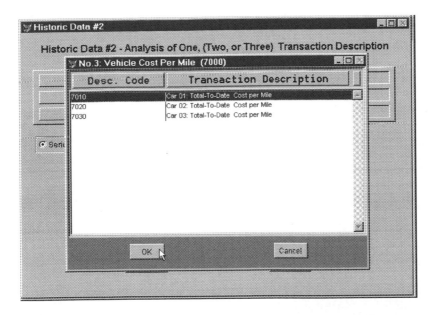

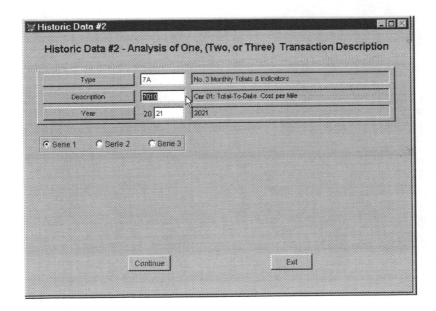

45

Printed in the United States
by Baker & Taylor Publisher Services